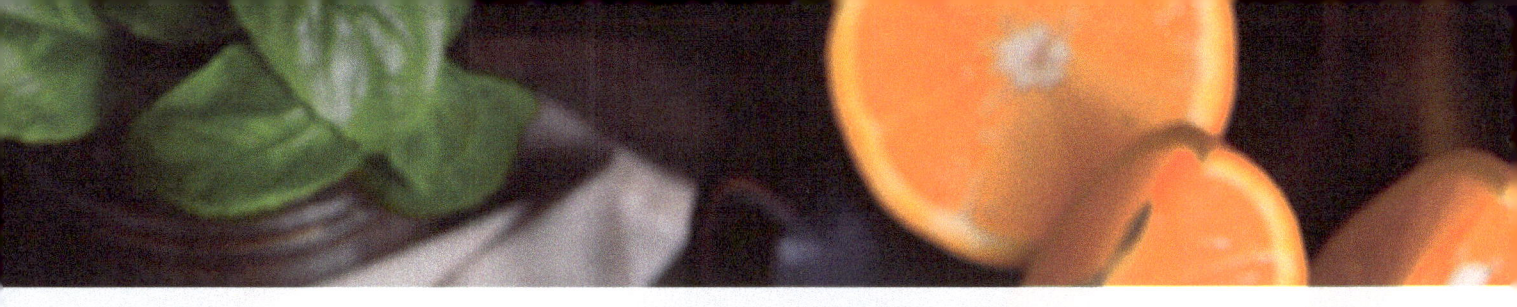

# NECESSARY GOODNESS

Delicious Cuisine for Gathering and Entertaining

# NECESSARY GOODNESS

## Delicious Cuisine for Gathering and Entertaining

Master Chef Charlie S. Redden • Eartha S. Dunston

Bob J. Nash • Janis F. Kearney

Necessary Goodness: Delicious Cuisine for Gathering and Entertaining

Recipes Copyright © 2023 J.D. Publishing House, LLC

All rights reserved. No part of this book may be reproduced or transmitted in any form or by any means, electronic or mechanical, including photocopying, recording or by any information storage and retrieval system, without permission in writing from the publisher, J.D. Publishing House, LLC.

First Edition 2023

Hardcover
ISBN: 978-0-9969302-5-3

Paperbook
ISBN: 978-0-9889644-9-5

Category page photo credits: Envato Elements
Creative Direction: EDC Creations Media Group

Printed in the United States of America

Get more updates and tour information at www.necessarygoodness.com

# FOREWORD

## Master Chef Charlie S. Redden, Jr.

Good food has brought families, friends, strangers and even enemies together throughout history – in celebrations, in goodbyes, in memorials, and for simple family gatherings. Good Food has created lasting memories, and as I look back over my life, I am proud that my last 35 years have been about creating lasting memories through my art and craft--cooking. My most recent achievement ranked as a Master Chef is a milestone I have worked toward my whole life, from that moment I entered the Culinary industry as a young man, not knowing where the journey might take me.

Human beings have always thrived on connections, family, and relationships. Unfortunately, the COVID pandemic changed life for most of us, as we found ourselves isolated, connected only by phones or social media, unable to come together and celebrate life and love as we have done since the beginning of time. Some of us, however, thrived during the world's "downtime."

For people like me, for whom cooking is an extension of who I am, social media allowed me to continue to express my love for food—the preparing, the explaining its origin, the online teaching—which helped relieve some of the stress of isolation during the pandemic. As life resumes some sense of normalcy, families are coming together once again—in church, school, family night, backyard cookouts, holiday season feasts, or just a simple bowl of soup shared over conversations and laughter.

With that in mind, I am proud to join like-minded food lovers and cooks to create this cookbook, *Necessary Goodness*. I hope you enjoy trying each recipe to share with friends, families and even strangers, to create unforgettable memories.

# Contents

13. CONTRIBUTORS

18. SOUPS, SALADS & CHILI

38. BREAD AND ROLLS

44. FISH AND SEAFOOD

58. DINNER & ENTREES

76. SIDE DISHES

94. DESSERTS

104. RESOURCES

# Contributors

# EARTHA S. DUNSTON

Eartha S. Dunston is an award-winning author and quintessential southern cook, known for creating simple cuisine often rooted deep in history with rich stories behind her dishes. She recalls, for example, standing, at the age of three, in a chair at the stove helping her father stir up a traditional southern breakfast. Her maternal grandparents were both professional cooks in Mobile, Alabama. Eartha grew up in kitchens where gumbo was made from fresh-caught Gulf seafood; and where homemade barbecue sauce rivaled the pit-smoked meat it was created for.

She has fond memories of picking fresh peaches, blackberries, and pecans for her mother to make pies. There are also vivid memories of playing on land with the backdrop of endless rows of a vegetable garden she helped plant. These are the memories, experiences and "planted seeds" that brought back to life years of buried skills she now uses to feed and entertain her family
and friends.

With a passion for everything arts and culture, Eartha was named the 2016 Black Pearls Magazine Literary Excellence Author of the Year award recipient for her debut Children's book, The Hair Adventures of Princess Lindsey Sidney. She is also a contributing author to Writing our Lives: A Southern Storytellers Anthology, where she shares a snippet of her forthcoming memoir, Chasing Dreams in the Midst of the Storm. Eartha also serves as an Advisory Board member on the Celebrate! Maya Project, a nonprofit dedicated to promoting literacy, creativity, and social consciousness of the life and work of literary icon, Dr. Maya Angelou.

Eartha holds a bachelor's degree from Alabama State University and a master's from Virginia Commonwealth University. She resides in the Washington, DC, area.

# BOB J. NASH

Former USDA Undersecretary, and Director of Presidential Personnel for the Clinton White House.

Bob J. Nash attended Booker T. Washington High School in Texarkana, Arkansas. He attended AM&N College in Pine Bluff, Arkansas, where he achieved his B.A. in Sociology. After college, he moved to Washington, DC, with a scholarship to Howard University. There, he received his master's in urban planning.

Bob grew up in the Southwest region where alligator, snake, gar, and lots of bayou fish were the norm. Bob learned to cook in the small cafes and grills of Texarkana, Arkansas, saying, "My big chance came when the fry cook called in sick; the owner knew he was drunk again. From that night on, I was the fry cook." Bob's specialties are southern cooked foods, including grilled meats, vegetables, southern fried catfish and, of course, Tex-Mex cornbread.

Bob worked 50 years in the nonprofit world, state government, federal government, and banking. He was vice president of the Winthrop Rockefeller Foundation; Economic Advisor to Governor Bill Clinton; then joined the Clinton White House, where he was appointed by President Clinton to serve as Undersecretary of USDA and as White House Director of Presidential Personnel.

He worked seven years as Vice Chair of Shore Bank Chicago before joining the Hillary Clinton Campaign in 2008. He later worked as a consultant for the Witt Emergency Services. Today, Bob is a self-employed consultant with Bob J. Nash & Associates.

# JANIS F. KEARNEY

Author, Publisher, and Former Personal Diarist to President Clinton.

Janis F. Kearney attended Gould High School, then attended the University of Arkansas in Fayetteville. She received a B.A. in Journalism, with a minor in English. Janis hails from the southeastern edge of Arkansas and grew up with the Mississippi/ Louisiana accents from her well-traveled father, and her mother, from southwest Arkansas.

Janis learned to appreciate Louisiana- tinged desserts from her father's jelly-rolls, caramel cakes, butter rolls and raisin bread, and from her mother, Ethel's lemon and coconut cakes, sweet potato pies, and teacakes. Her mother cooked just about anything moving to feed all 18 of us. Janis recalls biscuits that melted in her mouth and Ethel's Sunday morning fried chicken. In the kitchen, Janis finds the very same peace and tranquility her mother enjoyed. "The kitchen is where I feel my mother's presence most, hear her voice and recall her beautiful singing I woke to each and every morning."

Janis worked seven years in Arkansas state government before taking over as Managing Director of the Arkansas State Press newspaper, founded by civil right leader Daisy Gatson Bates. Janis purchased the newspaper in 1988. She served briefly in the Clinton White House Media Affairs department before being appointed as Assistant Administrator and Director of Public Communications for the U.S. Small Business Administration. For the last five years of the Clinton Administration, she served as Personal Diarist to President William J. Clinton. Janis began her career as writer and publisher in 2001 in Chicago. Today her life includes writing, serving as founder and publisher of WOW! Publishing, and as president of Celebrate! Maya Project, a nonprofit serving youth of the Arkansas Delta.

# MASTER CHEF CHARLIE S. REDDEN, JR.

Charlie Santoina Redden, Jr., recognized as Chef Charlie, is the first Certified Executive Chef in the history of the White House Presidential Food Service. A retired Navy Culinary Specialist, Chef Charlie was born in Florence, South Carolina, and raised in the tough streets of the East Riverside Projects in Wilmington, Delaware, where he also received his education. While attending Howard High School of Technology from 1974 – 1978, he was mentored about the food industry by Lucian Dillingham, who was the Commercial Food Instructor and is still one of the most influential and successful restaurant business owners in several international airport locations.

After graduating from high school, Charlie was selected from the top three students in his class to work at the Hotel Dupont in Wilmington, Delaware, under the strict training of Executive Chef Roland Johnson. Charlie learned not only the food service aspect of catering and food service procedures, but also a great deal about life and how to get ready for the real world. He shared his dreams and aspirations to be a chef with Executive Chef Johnson, who encouraged and taught him to always remember where he came from and how to consistently conduct himself as a young man in order to achieve his goals.

Chef Charlie took the lessons he learned from Dillingham and Executive Chef Johnson with him when he joined the Navy in 1980 as a culinary specialist preparing food for admirals, commodores, and captains. The last seven and a half years of his 21-year career were spent working at the White House.

From the time he reported, he was assigned the catering supervisor role, directly responsible for catered functions at the White House Mess. From October 1995 to November 1997, that meant preparing and setting up more than 600 catered events and receptions—by himself—for President Bill Clinton and his senior staff members. This feat had never been achieved in the history of the White House Culinary Specialist Program, especially not by one person.

Soup. Salad. Chili.

# Chef Charlie's Cream of Lobster and Crabmeat Soup

## Ingredients

- 1 pound of lobster, divided
- 1 pound jumbo lump crab meat, divided
- 1 pint milk
- 1 quart half and half
- 2 pints heavy whipping cream
- 1 tablespoon ground nutmeg
- ¼ cup butter
- ½ tablespoon shrimp bouillon
- ⅛ teaspoon pepper
- 1 tablespoon cornstarch
- 1 tablespoon ground ginger
- 1 teaspoon Old Bay Seasoning

## Directions

To create the soup, bring milk, half and half, and heavy whipping cream to a boil. Add half of the lobster and crab meat, nutmeg, ginger, Old Bay Seasoning, butter, salt, and pepper. When it starts to boil, make a paste of cornstarch, and cold water or cold chicken stock. Start by added the cornstarch to a small bowl and slowly whisking in the liquid until a paste forms. Whisk the paste into the soup to prevent lumps and whisk until the soup has thickened. If lumps do form, continue whisking until they have been whisked out. Add the rest of the lobster and crab meat. Stir gently to preserve the lumps of the lump crab meat. Heat thoroughly until crab and lobster are heated through. Soup should be semi thick. Add more Old Bay to taste and serve hot.

# Chef Charlie's Cream of Asparagus Soup with Grilled Salmon

**ASPARAGUS SOUP INGREDIENTS**
- 2 tablespoons powdered chicken bouillon
- 2 bunches asparagus (about 2 pounds)
- ½ cup extra-virgin olive oil
- ½ large white onion chopped
- 1 tablespoon garlic powder
- ½ cup heavy cream
- 3 cups whole milk
- 1 teaspoon salt
- Freshly ground black pepper for desired taste

**GRILLED SALMON INGREDIENTS**
- ½ cup olive oil
- ¼ cup lemon juice
- ½ teaspoon sea salt
- ⅛ teaspoon black pepper
- ⅛ teaspoon garlic powder
- 4 (6 ounces) salmon fillets

## ASPARAGUS SOUP DIRECTIONS

Take one bunch of the asparagus and cut into 1-inch pieces. The second bunch remains whole to be added in as garnish. In a medium saucepan, heat half of the olive oil. Add all asparagus and sauté until bright green and just tender, about 2 to 3 minutes. Season with 1 teaspoon salt and 1/8 teaspoon black pepper. Reserve the olive oil in the pan to later sauté the onions. When asparagus is tender, transfer to an ice bath with a slotted spoon. After cooling, separate the whole pieces from the 1-inch pieces. Sit aside for topping.

In the saucepan, add a little more olive oil. Sauté white onion and garlic powder over medium-heat until the onions are translucent; softened but not browned, about 3 minutes. Whisk in flour with onion and garlic powder to create a paste. Reduce heat to a low simmer. Add heavy cream and 3 cups of whole milk. Simmer for 5 minutes to allow flavors to meld and thicken. Remove from heat and let cool slightly. Season to taste with chicken bouillon. Add in 1-inch pieces of asparagus and stir gently. Add whole asparagus for garnish. Serve hot.

# Cream of Asparagus Soup with Grilled Salmon (con't)

**ASPARAGUS SOUP INGREDIENTS**
- 2 tablespoons powdered chicken bouillon
- 2 bunches asparagus (about 2 pounds)
- ½ cup extra-virgin olive oil
- ½ large white onion chopped
- 1 tablespoon garlic powder
- ½ cup heavy cream
- 3 cups whole milk
- 1 teaspoon salt
- Freshly ground black pepper

**GRILLED SALMON INGREDIENTS**
- ½ cup olive oil
- ¼ cup lemon juice
- ½ teaspoon sea salt
- ⅛ teaspoon black pepper
- ⅛ teaspoon garlic powder
- 4 (6 ounces) salmon fillets

## GRILLED SALMON DIRECTIONS

To create the marinade, combine olive oil, lemon juice, sea salt, black pepper, and garlic powder in a small bowl. Set aside ¼ cup of this marinade. Place salmon in a shallow dish and pour the remaining marinade over the top of the fish. Cover and refrigerate for 30 minutes. Remove the salmon and discard the used marinade. Preheat the outdoor grill for medium-heat and lightly oil the grate. Place salmon on the preheated grill, skin side down. Cook, basting occasionally with the reserved marinade, until the fish flakes easily with a fork, about 3-5 minutes on each side. Add grilled salmon to the side of soup bowl. Garnish and serve hot.

# Chef Charlie's Chicken Noodle Soup

## Ingredients

- 2 (6 ounce) cans of diced, cooked chicken breast
- 4 tablespoons of chicken bouillon to taste
- ½ teaspoon pepper
- 1 large onion, chopped
- 1 ½ tablespoons of garlic powder
- 10 cups of water
- 4 celery ribs, chopped
- ½ cup of baby cut carrots
- 1 teaspoon minced fresh thyme or ¼ teaspoon dried thyme
- 1 teaspoon of dried oregano
- 3 cups uncooked, fluffy, egg noodles (about 8 ounces)
- 1 tablespoon chopped fresh parsley
- 3 tablespoons of olive oil

## Directions

In a 6-quart stockpot, add olive oil. Bring to medium-heat adding onion, celery, carrots, thyme and oregano. Cook and stir over medium-high heat until tender, 4-5 minutes. Add water, bouillon and garlic powder to cooked vegetables. Stir gently. Simmer on medium heat for 1 minute longer. Stir to loosen browned bits from pan. Reduce heat adding noodles and cooked, diced, chicken breast. Let stand, covered, until noodles are tender, 5-10 minutes. If desired, adjust seasoning with salt and pepper and garnish with parsley.

# Chef Charlie's Cream and Mushroom Soup

## Ingredients

- 6 bread bowls
- 2 cups sliced portabella mushrooms
- ½ stick of salted butter
- 1 tablespoon garlic powder
- 3 tablespoon all-purpose flour
- 3 ½ cups vegetable/chicken broth
- 1 cup whole milk
- ½ cup cream
- Salt and black pepper to taste

## Directions

Slice portabella mushroom thinly. (I used a mixed of cremini and button mushrooms). Melt the butter in a heavy based sauce pan over low-heat. Add garlic powder and flour to butter. Keep stirring until it becomes a paste in about 1 minute. Toss in the mushrooms and season with salt and black pepper. Cook until the mushroom are soft. Pour in 3 cups of broth and stir. Reduce the heat and simmer gently for a few minutes, stirring occasionally. Pour in milk and bring to a medium boil. Pour in the cream and let it reheat gently for about 3-4 minutes. Remove from heat. Serve in the bread bowls.

# Chef Charlie's Texas Style Beef and Seven-Bean Chili

## Ingredients

- 1 tablespoon olive oil
- 1 large onions, chopped
- ½ cup of red bell pepper, chopped
- ½ cup of green pepper, chopped
- 2 tablespoons of roasted garlic, minced
- 3 ½ pounds ground beef (15% fat)
- 1 (16 ounce) can of each 7 cans total: light kidney beans, dark kidney beans, navy beans, black beans, northern beans, lentil beans, and pinto beans, drained
- 3 tablespoons beef powder bouillon
- 2 tablespoons ground cumin
- 1 teaspoon sweet paprika
- 1 (28 ounce) can of diced tomatoes in juice
- 1 cup of barbecue sauce
- Sour cream to taste
- Grated cheddar cheese
- Chopped green onions
- Chopped fresh cilantro
- Sliced banana peppers

## Directions

Heat oil in a heavy, large pot over medium-high heat. Add onions and peppers; sauté until brown, about 6 minutes. Add garlic and sauté 1 minute. Add ground beef and bouillon powder; sauté until brown, breaking up with the back of fork, about 5 minutes. Add chili powder, cumin, and paprika, then mix in tomatoes with juices, plus the 7 cans of beans and bring to boil. Reduce heat and simmer until chili thickens and flavors blend, stirring occasionally. Cook about 45 minutes. Skim any fat from the surface of the chili and add barbecue sauce. Ladle chili into bowls. Serve, adding desired topping from the bowls of sour cream, grated cheese, green onions, banana peppers and cilantro.

# Chef Charlie's Seafood Tri-colored Pasta Salad

## Ingredients

- 2 pounds tri-color pasta, cooked
- 1 ½ cups of red cherry tomatoes
- 2 teaspoons dried oregano
- 2 teaspoons diced pimentos
- 2 tablespoons of powdered chicken bouillon
- ½ pound cooked, unfrozen, medium shrimp, peeled and deveined
- 2 tablespoons olive oil
- 1 cup of solid white canned tuna
- Shredded parmesan cheese
- 1 cup each of diced red and green bell pepper
- 1 can (2 ¼ ounces) small pitted black olives, drained
- 1 ⅓ cups Italian salad dressing
- ¼ to ½ teaspoon garlic powder

## Directions

Cook pasta according to package directions. Drain pasta and transfer to a bowl. In skillet, sauté shrimp and tuna in olive oil for 1 minute. Drain and cool. Add Italian dressing to mix. Pour seafood mixture over cooked pasta. Toss to coat. Sprinkle with parmesan cheese if desired. Add the remaining ingredients: salt, pepper for desired taste, oregano, garlic powder, chicken bouillon, black olives, tomatoes, pimentos, red and green bell peppers. Stir until thoroughly mixed. Ready to serve.

# Janis' Ambrosia Salad

## Ingredients

- 3 cups cubed apples
- 3 cups cubed fresh pineapple
- 3 cups blueberries
- 4 bananas, sliced
- 1 cup shredded coconut
- 3 cups walnuts
- 1 (6 ounce) container yogurt
- 2 teaspoons lemon extract
- 1 (12 ounce) container frozen nondairy whipped topping, thawed

## Directions

In a large salad bowl, layer half of the apples, pineapple, bananas, blueberries, coconut, and walnuts. In a medium bowl, combine whipped topping, yogurt and lemon extract. Spoon whipped topping mixture on top of the first half of fruit mixture. Place the last half of the fruit mixture. Cover the second half of the fruit mixture with whipped topping mixture. Garnish with walnuts and coconut.

# Janis' Seven-Layer Salad

## Ingredients

- 4 cups loosely packed, torn romaine lettuce
- 1 cup brussels sprouts, chopped
- 2 cups frozen peas, thawed
- 1 red pepper, chopped
- 6 hard-boiled eggs, quartered
- 4 green onions, chopped
- 1 cup shredded sharp cheddar cheese
- 4 slices bacon, cooked, crumbled (1 cup of bacon bits will also work)
- ½ cup ranch dressing
- ½ cup sour cream

## Directions

Place half the lettuce at bottom of bowl. Cover lettuce with half of the seven ingredients (raw brussels sprouts first, then frozen peas, chopped red pepper, three hard-cooked eggs, green onions, cheddar cheese and crumbled bacon). Cover mixture with half of the ranch salad dressing and sour cream. Place second half of the 7-ingredient mixture in a bowl. Spread second half of salad dressing and sour cream on top, completely covering the top layer. Place eggs, cheese and bacon on top. Cover and refrigerate several hours or overnight. Serve as is or toss before serving.

# Bread & Rolls

# Bob's Southern Jalapeno-Onion Cornbread

## Ingredients

- 6 cups self-rising meal
- 2 cups white flour
- 1 can creamed corn
- 1 can whole kernel corn
- 2 cups vegetable oil
- 1 cup sour cream
- 2 cups whole milk
- 2 whole eggs
- 1 medium white onion, finely chopped
- 6 fresh jalapeno peppers, finely chopped

## Directions

Preheat oven to 350°F. Mix together meal, flour, sour cream, milk, and eggs together, stirring well. Mix onions, jalapeno, and corn together; pour into mixture. Place two six-inch greased skillets in the oven for two minutes. Remove skillets, fill with cornbread mixture, and place in the oven. Cook until brown, approximately 25-30 minutes. Remove from oven, cut into slices and serve hot.

# Aunt Dorothy's Sweet Butter Dinner Rolls

## Ingredients

- 4 cups all-purpose flour
- 2 large eggs, beaten
- 2 packages active dry yeast
- ½ cup milk
- ½ cup sugar
- 1 ½ tsp salt
- ¼ cup butter, melted
- ½ cup warm water (120°F or less)

## Directions

Heat milk to a low boil and remove from heat. Stir in sugar, salt and butter. Set aside and allow to cool to lukewarm. In a large bowl mix ½ cup warm water and yeast. Stir until dissolved. Stir in lukewarm milk mixture. Add beaten eggs. Stir in half the flour. Beat until smooth. Add remaining flour gradually, mixing as you go. Your dough should be elastic and slightly stiff but not dry. Turn dough out onto a floured board and knead until smooth and very elastic. This usually takes 7-9 minutes.

Butter the inside of a large mixing bowl. Put dough in bowl and turn dough over a couple of times to coat it all with the butter. Cover bowl and place in a warm place so it can rise. It will take about 1 ½ hours to double in bulk. At that time punch dough down and turn out onto a lightly floured board to shape. Shape and fill as desired. To make dinner rolls, pinch off about 2-3 tablespoons of dough and shape into a ball. Place each one in a buttered muffin tin or baking pan, ½ inch apart, do not crowd rolls.

Cover prepared rolls and allow to rise in a warm place until doubled in bulk, again about 1 hour. Rolls should not touch each other. (A little more rising will occur during baking). Preheat oven to 350°F when rolls are about 10 minutes from being ready to place in the oven. When ready to bake, place rolls in the warm oven and bake for 20-25 minutes. They should be browned nicely and smell so good and yeasty! Brush tops of rolls with melted butter when removed from the oven. Allow rolls to sit for at least 15-20 minutes before eating.

# Bob's Arkansas Delta Fried Catfish

## Ingredients

- 6 medium catfish filets
- 6 cups white cornmeal
- 1 cup white flour
- 2 teaspoons sea salt
- 2 teaspoons onion powder
- 2 teaspoons black pepper
- 2 cups lemon juice
- 1 quart vegetable oil
- 2 quarts water, room temperature

## Directions

Mix 2 cups of lemon juice in one gallon of water and submerge fish filets for six hours. Mix all dry ingredients together. Heat vegetable oil. Remove fish from water, pat dry. Completely immerse fish filets in cornmeal mixture. Place each filet in heated oil, turning as needed until fully cooked and browned, approximately three minutes. Place cooked fish on a paper towel. Eat while hot.

# Eartha's Easy Shrimp Creole

## Ingredients

- 1 pounds shrimp, raw and deveined
- 1 (8 ounce) can tomato sauce
- 1 (14 ounce) can of stewed tomatoes
- ½ cup diced, white onion
- ½ cup green bell pepper, chopped
- ¼ cup celery, chopped
- 3 cloves fresh garlic, chopped
- 2 bay leaves
- 3 tablespoons butter
- 1 tablespoon Worcestershire sauce
- 1 teaspoon chili powder
- ⅛ teaspoon cayenne pepper
- ½ teaspoon Old Bay Seasoning
- Salt to taste

## Directions

Heat butter to melt. Add diced onion, pepper, garlic, and celery. Cook until softened, about 5 minutes. Add cans of stewed tomatoes and tomato sauce. Add all dry seasoning, as well as bay leaves and Worcestershire sauce. Stir and simmer on low, about 15-20 minutes. Add shrimp and cook for another 5 minutes or so. Serve over a bed of cooked rice.

# Janis' Southern-fried Mackerel Croquet

## Ingredients

- 1 (14.75) can mackerel, drained
- 2 green onions, thinly diced
- ½ cup flour
- 2 eggs
- 1 teaspoon salt
- 1 teaspoon pepper
- ½ cup of vegetable oil
- 1 large onion, sliced

## Directions

Mix the mackerel, green onions, flour, eggs, salt and pepper in large bowl. Place large skillet on medium-heat, with vegetable oil. Form mixture into four patties. Add sliced onion to heating oil immediately before croquets are added. Place patties in hot oil, letting brown for 3-4 minutes, before turning. Drain on paper towel. Serve alone or on salad.

# Chef Charlie's Grilled Sword Fish Steaks with Mango Salsa

## Ingredients

- 4 (7 ounce) sword fish steaks
- 2 teaspoon lemon juice
- 1 teaspoon coriander
- ¾ teaspoon cumin
- ½ teaspoon ground ancho chile
- ½ teaspoon sweet Spanish paprika
- ¾ teaspoon of salt
- ½ teaspoon ground pepper
- ⅓ cup of extra virgin olive oil

## Directions

In a food processor, blend the olive oil, lemon juice, spices, salt and pepper for about 4 minutes or until well-combined thick paste. Pat the swordfish steaks dry and place them in a pan (or a dish with sides to it) and apply the marinade generously on both sides and set aside for 15 minutes or so while you heat the outdoor, gas grill. Preheat the gas grill on high at 350-400°F (oil the grates before using). When ready, grill the fish steaks on high-heat for 3 minutes on one side, turn over once and grill on the other side for 3 minutes or so (the fish should flake easily, while maintain firmness. You will likely see a bit of pink on the inside.

**Mango Salsa Instructions**
Combine 1 diced mango, 1 diced red bell pepper, ⅓ cup chopped red onion, 2 tablespoons each fresh lime juice and finely chopped fresh cilantro, ½ teaspoon ground ancho chile and a pinch of cayenne pepper in a medium bowl; season to taste with salt. The salsa can be covered and refrigerated for up to 4 hours.

**Suggested wines for those who drink:  Pink or Red Moscato**

# Chef Charlie's Grilled Surf and Turf

## Ingredients

- 3 pounds New York strip steaks
- 4 lobster tails
- 1 cup extra virgin olive oil
- 1 cup melted butter
- 2 teaspoons each of salt and pepper
- 1 teaspoon granulated garlic powder

## Directions

In a extra large bowl, whisk olive oil, melted butter, salt and pepper and garlic until well blended into a marinade. Slice the steak into ½-inch strips. Split the lobster tails in shell. Add both to marinade. Let beef and lobster marinate for 30 minutes. Place both meats on outdoor, gas grill set at 375-400°F until grill mark appear and beef and lobster are done. The beef should be juicy and not dry. Cook about 5-7 minutes. Cook lobster until flaky.

**Suggested wine for those who drink: Pinot Noir**

# Chef Charlie's Grilled Scallops with White Wine Sauce

## Ingredients

### Grilled Scallops Ingredients
- 1 pound scallops
- ¼ cup olive oil
- 3 garlic cloves, minced
- Salt and pepper
- Juice of one lemon

### White Wine Sauce Ingredients
- ½ cup butter
- 2 tablespoons all-purpose flour
- 1 teaspoon curry powder
- 10 fluid ounce white wine
- 9 fluid ounce fresh double cream
- Squeeze of lemon juice

## Directions

**Grilled Scallops Instructions**
In a medium sized bowl combine olive oil, lemon juice and garlic to create a marinade. Salt and pepper the scallops. Add to the bowl and toss in marinade to coat. Let marinate in the fridge for about 20 minutes. Place the scallops on a outdoor grill over medium-high heat at 375°F. Let cook on each side for about 2 minutes or until cooked throughout and slightly charred.

**White Wine Sauce Instructions**
Melt the butter in a pan and gently stir in all-purpose flour until dissolved. Add the wine, bring to the boil and boil rapidly for 10 minutes or until the liquid is reduced by half. Add the cream and mustard and warm through thoroughly. Add a squeeze of lemon juice and some black pepper. Serve sauce under the scallops.

**Suggested wine for those who drink: Light Chardonnay**

Dinner & Entrees

# Chef Charlie's Grilled Teriyaki Lamb Chops

## Ingredients

- 4 lamb chops
- ½ cup teriyaki sauce
- 1 teaspoon fresh rosemary
- ½ cup soy sauce
- ¼ cup water
- ¼ cup brown sugar
- 2 tablespoons sherry vinegar
- ½ tablespoon powdered ginger
- ½ tablespoon garlic powder

## Directions

Combine all ingredients in a saucepan and heat just until sugar and spices dissolve to create the marinade. Pour marinade over chops and let marinate for 10–20 minutes. Remove from marinade and cook on outdoor grill at 375°F for 3 minutes per side, depending on the heat of fire. Medium-well doneness will still have a little pink in the center. Read to serve.

**Suggested wine for those who drink:  Pinot Noir**

# Chef Charlie's Chicken and Sausage Gumbo
## (Low Liquid)

### Ingredients

- 7 tablespoons butter
- 4 cups of boiling water
- 5 tablespoons flour
- 1 cup sweet onion chopped
- 1 cup red bell pepper chopped
- 1 cup yellow bell pepper chopped
- 2 celery stalks chopped
- 2 cups sliced smoked beef sausage
- 1 ½ tablespoon garlic powder
- 1 teaspoon creole seasoning or cajun seasoning
- 4 tablespoons chicken bouillon
- 2 ½ cups chopped chicken breast
- 1 bay leaf
- 1 cup frozen okra
- 1 teaspoon ground black pepper
- 2 cups cooked white rice
- 1 teaspoon cayenne pepper
- 1 ½ teaspoons paprika

### Directions

Melt the butter in a large stock pot over medium-high heat. Whisk in the flour and continue whisking until the mixture starts to turn golden brown and smell nutty, approximately 4-5 minutes. Do not stop whisking or the roux will burn. Stir in the onion, bell peppers and celery. Continue cooking for 2-3 minutes, stirring constantly, until the vegetables begin to soften. Add the beef sausage to the pot and stir to combine. Cook for 1 minute longer. Stir in the garlic powder, cayenne, paprika and creole seasoning. Cook for 1 minute longer, stirring constantly and scraping up any brown bit on the bottom of the pan. Slowly add the chicken bouillon and hot boiling water to the pot stirring to combine. Add the chicken and bring the soup to a boil for 4-5 minutes. Turn the heat to low. Add the bay leaf, okra and pepper to the soup and stir to combine. Simmer for 10 minutes or until the soup begins to thicken. Serve the chicken gumbo over rice, if desired. Sprinkle with chopped green onions and parsley for an extra pop of color.

# Chef Charlie's Chicken Breast Stuffed with Lump Crabmeat

**LUMP CRAB MEAT**
- 4 boneless skinless chicken breast halves (about 1 pound)
- 1 pound jumbo lump crabmeat, cartilage removed
- ¾ cup whole milk
- 2 eggs
- ¼ cup chopped onion
- ¼ cup of red and green peppers
- ¾ cup of breadcrumbs
- 2 tablespoons minced, fresh parsley
- ½ teaspoon salt
- ½ teaspoon paprika
- Dash of pepper
- 8 wooden toothpicks

**WHITE WINE SAUCE**
- ¼ cup of all-purpose flour
- ¼ stick of unsalted butter
- 1 ½ cups of heavy cream
- 1 teaspoon of salt
- ½ cup of Chardonnay wine

## Directions

In a large bowl, stir all crab meat ingredients except chicken breasts. Place each half of the breast between plastic wrap and flatten chicken with a food service mallet to ¼-inch thickness. After removing plastic wrap, sprinkle a dash of salt and pepper on each side of chicken breast. Spoon about ½ cup of the crab mixture on each chicken breast. Roll up and secure with a toothpick. Place in a greased 9-inch square baking dish. Cover and bake at 350°F for 30 minutes or until chicken juices run clear. Now it's time to prepare white wine sauce while chicken breast is baking. Melt ½ stick of unsalted butter in a medium skillet on low-heat, whipping in all-purpose flour until dissolved, add heavy cream, salt and white wine until ingredients are well mixed into a medium-thick texture. Remove toothpicks from the cooked chicken breast and crab mixture rolls. Slice into ½ inch medallions and top with white wine sauce. Serve with buttered linguine if desired.

**Suggested wines for those who drink:  Pinot Gris or Chardonnay**

# Chef Charlie's Rainbow Bell Peppers Stuffed with Sautéed Curry Vegetables

## Ingredients

- 6 large bell peppers any color
- ½ cup of melted butter
- 2 tablespoons of mild curry powder
- 1 cup frozen corn
- 1 (15 ounce) can black beans, rinsed
- 1 pound frozen mixed vegetables
- 10 ounces frozen, chopped cauliflower
- 1 (14 ounce) can diced tomatoes, drained
- 2 tablespoons fresh cilantro or parsley, chopped
- Salt and ground black pepper

## Directions

In a large stock pot, bring 4 quarts of water and 1 tablespoon salt to boil. Trim ½-inch from the top of each pepper and remove the stem and seeds. Add peppers to the water and cook until they begin to soften, about 3 minutes. Remove from water and place cut-side up to cool. Meanwhile, preheat the oven to 350°F. Heat butter in a large skillet over medium-high heat until shimmering. Add mixed vegetables, chopped cauliflower and curry powder. Cook until softened for about 5 minutes. Add corn and black beans; stir until heated through. Pour into a large bowl. Add tomatoes and cilantro to the large bowl with the black beans and stir to combine. Place the peppers in a 9" x 9" baking dish. Divide the filling evenly among the peppers. Bake until the filling is hot, about 30 minutes.

# Grilled Beef Tenderloin with Grilled Vegetables

## Ingredients

**Beef Tenderloin Seasoning**
- 4 (6 ounce) beef tenderloin medallions
- 2 cups extra virgin olive oil
- 2 teaspoons salt
- ½ teaspoon pepper

**Grilled Vegetables Seasoning**
- ¼ teaspoon salt
- 1 cup extra virgin olive oil
- ¼ teaspoon ground black pepper
- Whole asparagus, cleaned
- Sliced red and green peppers
- Shiitake mushrooms
- Pre-boiled small potatoes, sliced

## Directions

Preheat grill to 375-400°F. Cook meat and vegetable on grill at the same time. Coat the 4 tenderloin beef steaks with olive oil. Sprinkle with salt and pepper. Let marinate for 5 minutes. Place tenderloin on grill and grill for 4 minutes on each side until medium well. In a large bowl, mix all vegetables and cooked, sliced potatoes together. Toss in olive oil. Season with salt and pepper. Place in a grill pan. Put the pan on the grill and cook until grill marks appear. Meat and vegetables are ready to serve.

**Suggested wines for those who drink:  Beaujolais by Louis Jadot or Merlot**

# Chef Charlie's Grilled Juicy Beef Burgers

## Ingredients

- ½ cup red and green peppers mixed
- 1 pound (90-percent) lean ground beef divide into 4 parts
- 4 slices pepper jack cheese
- 6 slices of cooked bacon (optional)
- Beef bouillon
- Freshly ground black pepper
- 4 medium size hamburger buns, split
- Vegetable oil or nonstick grilling cooking spray

## Directions

Heat the outdoor grill to medium-high heat and lightly oil the grates using a paper towel soaked in vegetable oil or nonstick grilling cooking spray. In a medium sized bowl, mix the red and green peppers into the beef. Add in beef bouillon and pepper. Shape into round patties. Place each patty on the grill and cook 2 ½ minutes on each side; flipping as needed. Lightly butter and toast the opened hamburger buns on the grill. Place one bun on each plate. Adding bacon is optional. Put the hamburgers, buns and pepper jack cheese together and serve with condiments of choice.

# Chef Charlie's Ultimate Philly Cheesesteak

## Ingredients

- ½ red pepper, sliced
- 4 button portabella mushrooms, sliced
- 2 tablespoons unsalted butter, divided
- 2 eight inch hoagie rolls, sliced
- ½ green bell pepper, sliced
- ½ onion, sliced
- 4 button mushrooms, sliced
- 16 ounces tenderloin steak, thinly sliced
- 2 teaspoons Worcestershire sauce
- 4 slices white provolone cheese
- Salt and pepper to taste

## Directions

In a sauté pan over medium-heat, add 1 tablespoon of butter. Once melted, add bell peppers, onions and mushrooms; stirring occasionally, until veggies are lightly browned and onions turn translucent. Remove from pan and set aside. Season sliced tenderloin with salt and pepper. Add 1 tablespoon of butter to pan. Once melted add tenderloin to skillet and cook for 2-4 minutes, flipping occasionally. Add Worcestershire sauce to skillet and stir to combine. Reduce heat to low. Return veggies to pan and stir to combine. Split your steak mixture in half on either side of the pan. Lay two pieces of cheese onto each half and allow to melt, about 1 minute. Optionally, butter insides of hoagie rolls with 1 tablespoon of butter and toast. Spoon cheesesteak mixture into your hoagie rolls. Serve immediately.

# Chef Charlie's Baked Southern Style Turkey Wings

## Ingredients

- 2 ½ pounds turkey wings cut into sections, if bought whole
- 2 tablespoon olive oil, you can substitute it with vegetable oil
- 1 teaspoon garlic powder
- 1 tablespoon onion powder
- 2 tablespoons powder chicken bouillon broth
- 2 ½ cups turkey or chicken broth or even water

## Directions

Preheat oven to 350°F.  Wash and clean the turkey wings. Next, place the wings into a large bowl or dish and drizzle the wings with the olive oil. Sprinkle all of the seasoning onto the wings, then rub the seasonings all over the wings. Remove the wings from the bowl and place them into a oiled baking dish. In the bowl that the wings were in, there will be leftover seasonings. Pour 2 ½ cups of broth or water into the bowl, stir, then pour the broth or water into the baking dish with the wings. Cover the baking dish and cook the wings in the oven on 350°F, for about 1 ½ hours to 2 hours. Uncover the wings and bake uncovered for about 15-20 minutes until golden brown. Serve over buttered rice with a side of seasoned butter beans.

Side Dishes

# Janis' "Yellow, not White" Potato Salad

## Ingredients

- 5-7 boiled large potatoes
- 5 hard-boiled eggs
- 14 ounce sandwich spread (not mayonnaise)
- 12 or 14 ounces pickle relish
- 1 tablespoon apple cider vinegar
- 1 teaspoon sugar
- 2 tablespoon yellow mustard

## Directions

Boil potatoes until hulls are easily peeled, approx. 45 minutes; then set for 10 minutes in cool water. Boil 4-5 eggs for 20 minutes, let cool, then peel. Peel potatoes, place in large bowl. Add the sandwich spread, pickle relish, apple cider vinegar, mustard, sugar and cubed boiled eggs to the potatoes. Stir loosely with large mixing or serving spoon until a little chunky, but mostly smooth. Cover and refrigerate for at least 30 minutes to an hour before serving.

# Eartha's Bourbon Baked Beans and Smoked Sausage

## Ingredients

- 1 (28 ounce) can Bush's® Baked Beans, any variety
- 4 thick slices Applewood Smoked Bacon, chopped
- ½ pound smoked sausage links (Conecuh Hickory Smoked Sausage is good)
- ¼ large white onion, finely chopped
- ¼ cup dark brown sugar
- 2 tablespoons bourbon
- 1 teaspoon cinnamon
- ⅛ teaspoon cayenne pepper

## Directions

Preheat oven to 350°F. Cook bacon and sausage in a frying pan on medium-high heat, tossing occasionally until lightly browned, 4-5 minutes. Remove from frying pan and set aside. Pour off most of the excess pan drippings. Reduce heat to low setting. Cook onions in the same pan until translucent, 3-4 minutes. In a large bowl, add beans, brown sugar, cayenne, cinnamon, sausage, bacon, onions, and bourbon. Mix well. Bake about 45 minutes in a casserole dish.

# Eartha's Bahamian Macaroni and Cheese

## Ingredients

- 1 pound elbow macaroni
- 24 ounce shredded, sharp cheddar cheese
- 12 ounce can evaporated milk
- 2 eggs, well beaten
- 2 tablespoons pure butter
- ½ green bell pepper, finely chopped
- 2 tablespoons white onion, finely chopped
- ½ tsp cayenne pepper or 1 habanero finely chopped
- 1 teaspoon paprika
- Salt to taste

## Directions

Preheat oven to 350°F. Butter a 13x9-inch casserole dish and set aside. Cook macaroni per package instructions. Drain and return to pot (turn pot off). Add butter to the hot macaroni and stir to distribute evenly. Add peppers, onions, half the cheese and stir. Slowly add milk, stirring to incorporate all ingredients. Add paprika and cayenne pepper. Lastly, add the beaten eggs and stir. Pour mixture in casserole dish and sprinkle evenly with remaining cheese. Bake for 40-45 minutes. Let cool for at least 15 minutes. Cut into squares and serve warm.

# Eartha's Creamy Cheese Grits

## Ingredients

- 1 cup old-fashioned grits
- 2 cups chicken broth
- 2 cups water
- 6 ounces shredded extra-sharp cheese
- ½ cup heavy cream
- 1 tablespoon pure butter
- Salt and pepper to taste

## Directions

In a pot, bring chicken stock and water to a boil. Add grits slowly, stirring continuously. Reduce heat to low and let simmer for about 15 minutes. Stir occasionally. Stir in heavy cream, cheese and butter until cheese is melted and the grits are smooth and creamy. Serve immediately or cover and place grits on warm setting, stirring occasionally. Add broth, water or milk as needed to keep grits from becoming stiff. Sprinkle grits with a little cayenne pepper for a kick.

# Eartha's Fried Cabbage and Smoked Sausage

## Ingredients

- 1 head of cabbage, chopped
- 1 pound well-seasoned, smoked sausage cut into ½ inch rings (the Conecuh brand is good)
- 2 slices of bacon, chopped
- 1 white onion, chopped
- 1 teaspoon onion powder
- 1 teaspoon salt
- ½ teaspoon garlic powder
- ¼ cup water or chicken broth, if needed
- ½ red bell pepper, chopped
- Optional black pepper to taste

## Directions

Fry chopped bacon until it starts to brown, about 4 minutes. Add the chopped onion and continue to sauté until onions become translucent. Begin to add cabbage, stopping to stir and coat with the bacon and onion as you go along. You may have to wait a few minutes for it to cook down before adding more. Add ¼ cup of water or chicken broth to prevent sticking if needed. Once all the cabbage has been added, add all dry spices. Stir and cook on medium-heat until cabbage reaches desired tenderness, and most of the liquid has evaporated. You can add ½ red bell pepper for an additional flavor boost. This dish is excellent alone or over a bed of rice with a slice of homemade cornbread.

# Chef Charlie's Southern Fried Potatoes with Onion & Peppers

## Ingredients

- 3-4 medium size potatoes
- 1 medium onion, sliced
- ½ cup oil or shortening
- ½ cup red and green bell peppers, sliced
- 1 tablespoon bacon grease or ½ stick of unsalted butter
- Salt and black pepper to taste

## Directions

Wash and dry potatoes. Peel if desired. Slice the potatoes into ¼ inch thick slices. Place a skillet over medium-heat on your stove top. When skillet is hot, add the oil and the bacon grease. Bacon grease is optional. If you are using butter, add later in process. When the oil is hot, carefully add the potatoes. Add black pepper to taste, as desired. Stir potatoes, red and green peppers and sliced onions to coat in the oil or butter. Cover the skillet and let potatoes cook 10 minutes, stirring once halfway through. Remove lid. Cook uncovered for about 5 more minutes. Add salt to taste.

# Chef Charlie's Southern Style Seasoned Collard Greens

## Ingredients

- 2 pounds smoked turkey necks
- Sliced red peppers
- 2 medium-size sweet onions, sliced
- 3 (32 ounce) containers beef broth
- 4 quarts of water
- 3 (1 pound) packages fresh collard greens, washed and trimmed
- ⅓ balsamic vinegar
- 1 tablespoon brown sugar
- 1 stick of salted butter
- ¾ teaspoon black pepper

## Directions

Cook turkey necks in water over medium-heat in a stockpot for 2–3 hours or until soft. Watch pot and add water as needed through the cooking process. When done, drain off the water and set the turkey aside. In a medium stockpot add beef broth and collard greens. Boil over medium-high heat for about 3-4 hours or until greens are tender. Add onion, butter, sliced red peppers, balsamic vinegar, brown sugar and black pepper to cooked greens. Add turkey necks to this pot and reduce heat to low-simmer and cook for 10 minutes. Ready to serve.

# Chef Charlie's Fried Green Tomatoes

## Ingredients

- 2 cups peanut oil
- 6 green tomatoes, cut into ¼ inch rings
- Sea salt and freshly ground black pepper to taste
- ¾ cup all-purpose flour
- ½ cup of milk
- 1 ½ tablespoons garlic powder
- 5 eggs
- 1 ½ cups panko bread crumbs
- Desired choice of ranch or marinara dipping sauce

## Directions

In a deep-fryer, preheat oil to 350°F. Season tomatoes, on both sides, with sea salt and pepper. Place flour and garlic powder in a shallow dish. In another shallow dish, beat eggs with the milk. In another dish, mix bread crumbs. Dredge tomatoes through the flour, then the eggs, and then through the bread crumbs. Add only a few pieces to the fryer at a time, so they can cook evenly, about 2-3 minutes. Drain on paper towels and serve with your choice of dipping sauce.

Desserts

# Janis' Pumpkin Bread Pudding with Lemon Icing

## Ingredients

- Cooking spray
- 6 cups cubed whole wheat bread
- 2 cups half-and-half
- 1 (15 ounce) can pumpkin filling, pureed
- 1 ½ cups white sugar
- 3 eggs
- ½ cup raisins or craisins
- ½ cup walnuts
- 3 tablespoons butter, melted
- 2 teaspoons pumpkin pie spice
- 1 teaspoon grated lemon zest

## Directions

Preheat the oven to 350°F. Lightly grease a 7x11-inch baking dish with cooking spray. Place bread cubes in the greased baking dish and pour half and half on top. Mix pureed pumpkin, sugar, eggs, raisins, walnuts, butter, pumpkin pie spice and lemon zest into a large bowl. Pour over bread. Bake in the preheated oven until middle is set and edges are golden, about one hour. Remove from oven to cool.

**REAL SIMPLE LEMON ICING INGREDIENTS**
1 cup confectioners' sugar
1 ½ cups lemon juice
¼ cup lemon zest

**LEMON ICING DIRECTIONS**
Cook together on medium-heat until boiling and congealed to syrup. Drip icing atop cooling bread pudding.

# Chef Charlie's Banana Pudding Topped with Granola

## Ingredients

- 3 cups cold milk
- 1 teaspoon of imitation rum
- 1 teaspoon of vanilla extract
- 2 packages (3.4 ounce each) JELL-O Vanilla Flavor Instant Pudding
- 2 packages (3.4 ounce each) JELL-O Banana Flavor Instant Pudding
- 2 boxes vanilla wafers
- 4 bananas, sliced
- ½ cup of your favorite granola cereal, if desired
- 1 tub (8 ounce) COOL WHIP Whipped Topping, thawed

## Directions

Beat pudding mixes and milk with whisk 2 minutes. Let stand 5 minutes. Arrange half the wafers on bottom and continue up the sides of a large serving dish. Layer the mixture with the pudding mix and sliced bananas, then vanilla wafers. Repeat for all layers until you reach the top. End the layering with the pudding last. Cover with COOL WHIP; topped with granola. Refrigerate 3 hours. Serve cold.

# Chef Charlie's American Apple Pie Topped with French Vanilla Ice Cream

## Ingredients

- ¾ cup sugar
- ½ cup packed brown sugar
- 3 tablespoons all-purpose flour
- 1 teaspoon ground cinnamon
- ¼ teaspoon ground ginger
- ¼ teaspoon ground nutmeg
- 6 to 7 cups Granny Smith apples, peeled and thinly sliced
- 1 tablespoon lemon juice
- 2 deep dish frozen pie crusts
- 1 tablespoon butter
- 2 large egg whites
- Additional sugar for garnish

## Directions

Preheat oven to 375°F. In a medium bowl, combine the sugars, flour and spices; set aside. In a large bowl, toss apples with lemon juice. Add sugar mixture, toss to coat. Line a 9-inch pie plate with bottom crust; trim even with edge. If desired, place crust in the oven about 15 minutes or until slightly brown, remove and cool about 5 minutes. Fill with apple mixture; dot with butter. Roll remaining crust to fit top of pie, place over filling. Trim, seal and flute edges. Cut slits in top of crust. Beat egg white until foamy, brush over crust. Sprinkle with sugar. Cover edges loosely with foil. Bake at 375°F for 20 minutes. Remove foil and bake until crust is golden brown and filling is bubbly, 20-25 minutes longer. Cool on a wire rack. Top with your favorite French vanilla ice cream and drizzle with hot caramel, if desired.

# Resources

# Grocery List

| FRUITS & VEGETABLES | DAIRY | MEAT & FISH |
|---|---|---|
| | | |
| | | |
| | | |
| | | |
| | | |
| | | |
| | | |
| | | |

| BAKERY & BREAD | PANTRY | FROZEN |
|---|---|---|
| | | |
| | | |
| | | |
| | | |
| | | |
| | | |
| | | |
| | | |

| DRINKS | CLEANING | PERSONAL CARE |
|---|---|---|
| | | |
| | | |
| | | |
| | | |
| | | |
| | | |
| | | |
| | | |

| OTHER | NOTES/ REMINDERS |
|---|---|
| | |
| | |
| | |
| | |

# Grocery List

| FRUITS & VEGETABLES | DAIRY | MEAT & FISH |
|---|---|---|
| | | |

| BAKERY & BREAD | PANTRY | FROZEN |
|---|---|---|
| | | |

| DRINKS | CLEANING | PERSONAL CARE |
|---|---|---|
| | | |

| OTHER | NOTES/ REMINDERS |
|---|---|
| | |

# Meal Planner

WEEK OF: _____

|       | BREAKFAST | LUNCH | DINNER |
|-------|-----------|-------|--------|
| MON   |           |       |        |
| TUE   |           |       |        |
| WED   |           |       |        |
| THURS |           |       |        |
| FRI   |           |       |        |
| SAT   |           |       |        |
| SUN   |           |       |        |

WEEK OF: _____

|  | BREAKFAST | LUNCH | DINNER |
|---|---|---|---|
| MON | | | |
| TUE | | | |
| WED | | | |
| THURS | | | |
| FRI | | | |
| SAT | | | |
| SUN | | | |

WEEK OF: _____

| | BREAKFAST | LUNCH | DINNER |
|---|---|---|---|
| MON | | | |
| TUE | | | |
| WED | | | |
| THURS | | | |
| FRI | | | |
| SAT | | | |
| SUN | | | |

# Meal Planner

WEEK OF: _____

|  | BREAKFAST | LUNCH | DINNER |
|---|---|---|---|
| MON |  |  |  |
| TUE |  |  |  |
| WED |  |  |  |
| THURS |  |  |  |
| FRI |  |  |  |
| SAT |  |  |  |
| SUN |  |  |  |

# Meal Planner

WEEK OF: _____

|  | BREAKFAST | LUNCH | DINNER |
|---|---|---|---|
| MON | | | |
| TUE | | | |
| WED | | | |
| THURS | | | |
| FRI | | | |
| SAT | | | |
| SUN | | | |

# Meal Planner

WEEK OF: _____

|       | BREAKFAST | LUNCH | DINNER |
|-------|-----------|-------|--------|
| MON   |           |       |        |
| TUE   |           |       |        |
| WED   |           |       |        |
| THURS |           |       |        |
| FRI   |           |       |        |
| SAT   |           |       |        |
| SUN   |           |       |        |

# Notes & Reminders

## NOTES

# Notes & Reminders

## NOTES

# FOLLOW US ON SOCIAL MEDIA FOR MORE RECIPES

www.necessarygoodness.com

 @necessarygoodness   @necessarygoodness   @necessarygoodness

# NECESSARY GOODNESS

## Delicious Cuisine for Gathering and Entertaining

www.ingramcontent.com/pod-product-compliance
Lightning Source LLC
Chambersburg PA
CBHW061353010526
44107CB00011B/925